The Hidden Life of the
POND

Photographs by DWIGHT KUHN
Text by DAVID M. SCHWARTZ

CROWN PUBLISHERS, INC.
NEW YORK

To my children—Michele, Anne, David, and Brian.
D.K.

For my friends Leo and Jane, who have always
looked below the surface.
D.M.S.

Concept development and photo/editorial coordination
by the Soderstrom Publishing Group Inc.

Published by Crown Publishers, Inc., 225 Park Avenue South, New York, New
York 10003 and represented in Canada by the Canadian MANDA Group
Limited

CROWN is a trademark of Crown Publishers, Inc.

Manufactured in Japan

Book design by Kathleen Westray and Ed Sturmer

Library of Congress Cataloging-in-Publication Data

Kuhn, Dwight. The hidden life of the pond/ photographs by Dwight Kuhn;
text by David M. Schwartz.

Summary: Photographs and text introduce the animals, insects, and plants in
a pond.

1. Pond fauna—Juvenile literature. 2. Pond plants—Juvenile literature. 3. Pond
ecology—Juvenile literature. [1. Pond animals. 2. Pond plants. 3. Pond
ecology. 4. Ecology.] I. Schwartz, David M. II. Title.
QL146.3.S38 1988   574.5′26322   88-11863
ISBN 0-517-57060-2

10 9 8 7 6 5 4 3 2 1

First Edition

Bullfrog

As snow melts and winter slowly ends, a hidden world is coming to life. Many frogs, like this large bullfrog, wriggle out of the deep mud where they spent the winter. Warming temperatures and spring rains tell plants and animals that spring is here again.

Yellow-spotted salamander

The salamander spent its winter in the woods. In the spring, it heads to the pond where it grew up. Spring is the time when many creatures in the wild give birth. After a nose-rubbing courtship dance with her mate, a female salamander releases eggs into the pond, sometimes as many as two hundred at once.

Inside the eggs, the young salamanders look very much like tiny fish. Living off the yolk stored within the egg, they develop and grow. Microscopic plants called algae grow on the eggs and tint them green.

Salamander eggs

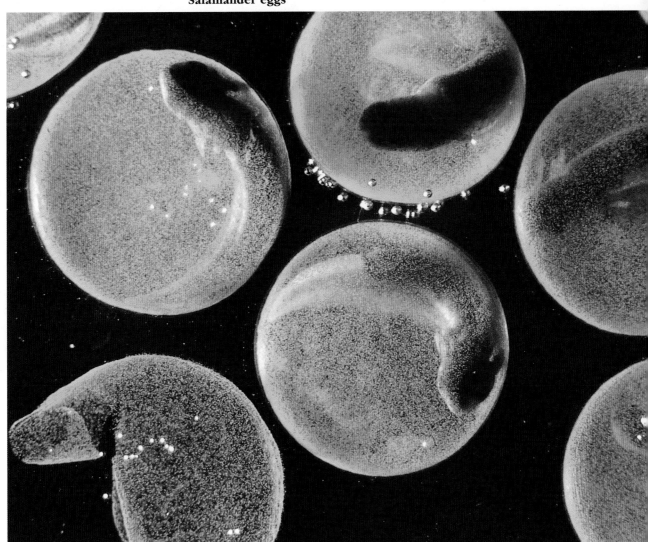

Mallard duck and ducklings

Colored a dull, speckly brown, the female mallard is leading her newly hatched brood of downy ducklings. A mallard drake, the male, takes no part in caring for the young, and that's a good thing for the ducklings. Their father's bright green head might attract predators.

Mallard drake

Belted kingfisher

A kingfisher keeps a sharp lookout over all the pond's activity. The bird can spot a small fish and swoop down from a tree to pluck it out of the water. Returning to its perch, the kingfisher stuns the fish by striking it against the branch.

Kingfishers establish their own hunting grounds. Their rattling cry says, "Keep away!" to other birds.

Water mite

Much less noticeable than the kingfisher, the fire-red water mite lives among the pond's vegetation. Only one-tenth of an inch long, this eight-legged relative of the spider uses long hairs on its legs to paddle through the water. Like the flea that attaches itself to a dog, the water mite hitches a ride on insects, worms, and other pond creatures. It feeds by slowly sucking their juices through its long, sharp beak.

Next to the water mite, the creature on the opposite page is a giant. Call it a crayfish, crawdad, crawfish, mud bug, or any of half a dozen other names....

This pond-bottom dweller is a miniature version of the lobster. From three to five inches in length, adult crayfish eat a wide variety of foods, including small fish and partly rotted plants that would otherwise fill up our ponds.

The female crayfish carries her eggs beneath her tail. Even after hatching, the babies will cling to their mother. Wherever she goes, they go!

Crayfish

Crayfish tail with young

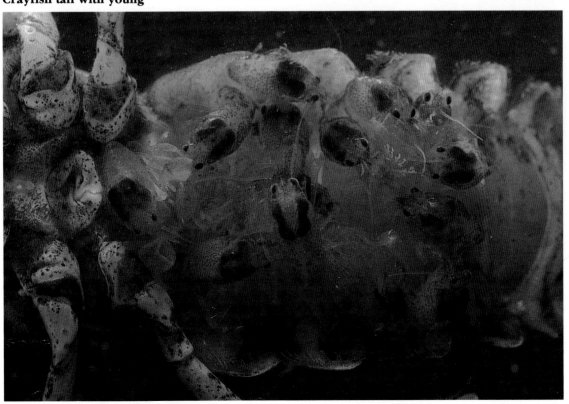

Like the crayfish, the catfish also eats
many little bits of plant and animal matter
that would build up and make the pond
an unpleasant place. With its barbels,
long fleshy whiskers that help it find
food, a catfish is well adapted to feeding
on the bottom of the pond.

Catfish

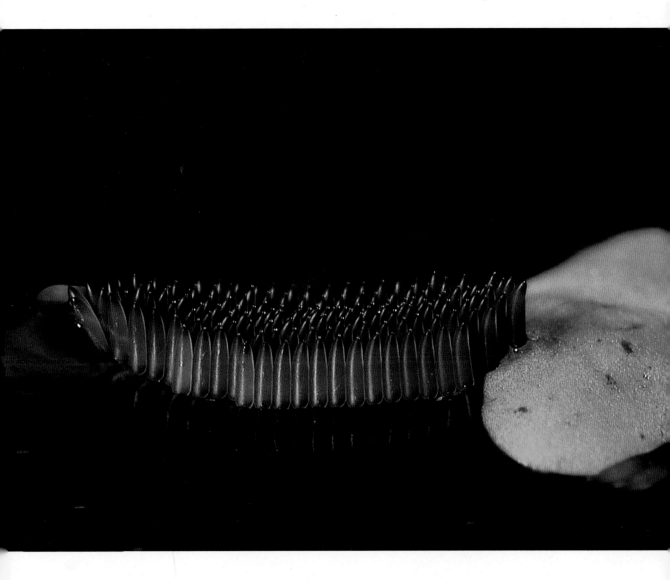

You may not recognize this curious floating mass, but just wait. It is a raft of eggs on the surface of the pond—the first stage in the life of an insect everybody knows.

A trapdoor opens at the bottom of each egg and a wriggling larva drops straight down into the water.

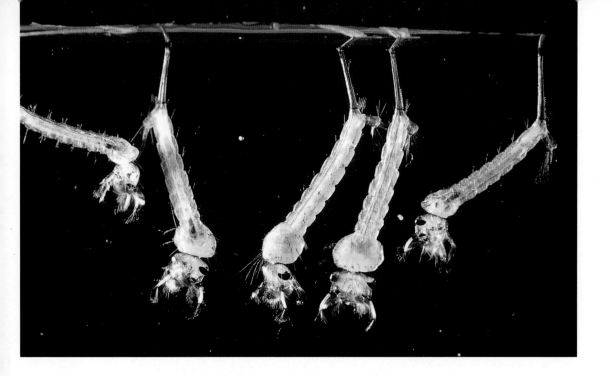

One end of the creature's body has a slender breathing tube that rises to pierce the water's surface. At the other end, feathery brushes send a stream of food and water into the larva's mouth.

After a few weeks, the larva forms a hard case around itself. This third stage in an insect's life is called a pupa. When it is ready to hatch, out comes an adult.

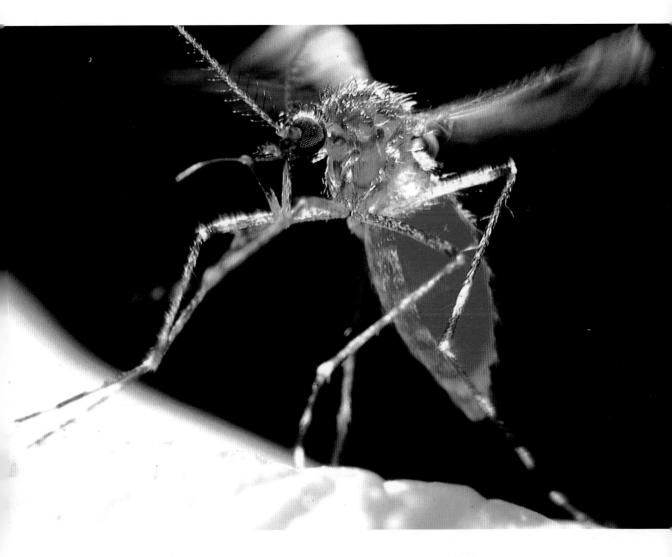

Now the insect is easy to identify. It's a mosquito!
Mosquitoes can beat their wings two hundred
fifty to five hundred times a second, creating a
high-pitched hum. While males eat only flower
nectar, females need to nourish their eggs with a
meal of blood. They find it under the skin of
unwilling victims like you!

White-tailed deer

Also a victim of the mosquito bite, the white-tailed deer wades into the shallows to drink water and munch vegetation. Always exciting to see, deer are shy and quick to run. The best time to catch a glimpse of them is early in the morning or just after sunset.

The pond also serves as drinking bowl and hunting ground for the raccoon, black-masked raider of the water's edge.

Raccoons eat nearly anything: frogs, fish, berries, crayfish, duck eggs, insects, plant roots. Often they use their agile paws to dunk food in the water. Raccoons are active mostly at night. By daylight, all you are likely to see are five-toed tracks in the mud.

Raccoon

By midsummer, spears
of slender-stalked cattails
fringe the pond. Cattail
leaves are able to bend and
twist without breaking, even
in the strongest breeze. At
this time of year, the cattails
have reached a height of six
feet or more, but they have
not yet sent up the flowering
spikes that will be so easy
to spot a month from now.

This fish has many names including sunfish, sunny, bluegill, and pumpkinseed. Sunfish are so common that thousands may live in a small pond.

Sunfish

Water strider

The water strider stands right on the water. Its large flat feet are lined with a velvety coating of waxy hairs that repel the water. This amazing insect can walk, run, skate, and skim across the water in search of prey, and it can leap six inches into the air. In human terms, this would be like jumping from the surface of the water to the roof of a house five stories tall!

Water bug

Dragonfly nymph

The giant water bug is among the pond's most fearsome inhabitants. These ferocious predators— some as long as three inches—snare small fish, tadpoles, and insects with their forelegs, then inject a poison that turns their victims' insides to a kind of soup. The water bug sucks up the liquid through its beak. Some kinds of water bugs care for their eggs in an interesting way. The female cements the eggs to the back of the male, who carries them until the young hatch and swim away.

The dragonfly nymph strikes by uncurling its long lower lip, which shoots out like a missile. At the tip of the lip are sharp hooks that clamp down on food and draw it into the nymph's jaws. Here, the meal is a tadpole.

Eventually, the well-fed nymph crawls up a stone or stalk until it is clear of the water. Its skin splits open and out crawls a winged adult. At first, the folded wings are thin and soft.

Adult dragonfly emerging from skin

Dragonfly

Gradually, the wings expand and harden, showing their glistening color pattern. In about twelve hours, adult dragonflies are ready to take to the air, never again to go underwater. Instead they will become a common sight above the pond's waters, zooming this way and that, looking for meals in the air.

When you think of a predator, you probably think of an animal that eats other animals. But along the moist, boggy banks of some ponds, a few plants capture living prey.

Sticky syrup-tipped hairs of the sundew attract insects and then "catch" them like fly-paper. The insect will dissolve in the plant's digestive juices, providing it with nourishment to grow.

The fragrant water lily also attracts insects, but it does not lure them to their death. Dozens of small pond animals live on, under, and inside the water lily's flowers, leaves, and stems.

Sundew

Water lily

By late summer, the cattails have sent up their flowering stalks, each bearing a cluster of dark brown flowers beneath smaller, lighter-colored flowers. The dark flowers will mature into thousands of tiny seeds packed in a velvety head that looks like a fat brown cigar.

Cattail in late summer

Star-nosed mole

One of the pond's most unusual-looking creatures is the star-nosed mole. Like other moles, it is nearly blind and uses its large scaly forefeet for burrowing underground.

But unlike other moles, it sometimes tunnels from the land into the water. It uses twenty-two sensitive feelers around its nose to help find tadpoles and worms on the bottom.

Like fingers, the feelers grasp the food and the mole carries it ashore. Though it's a fine swimmer and a skilled underwater hunter, the star-nosed mole eats on dry land.

Spring peeper tadpole

Every summer, in every pond, one of nature's most dramatic transformations takes place. Swimming with its long flattened tail, a spring peeper tadpole uses gills to breathe and a small rasplike tongue to scrape tiny plants off the rocks.

The first sign of change is the growth of legs. The eyes move toward the top of the head and the mouth widens as newly formed jaws push forward.

As the legs continue to grow and the tail shrinks, the creature becomes half tadpole, half frog. It still uses gills to breathe, but a nose and lungs are forming.

This fully grown spring peeper breathes air and hops on land. Bulging eyes home in on flying insects that the frog's long, sticky tongue will snare.

Spring peeper frog

Turtles evolved from an ancient group of reptiles that roamed the earth two hundred million years ago—before the first dinosaurs. A protective shell has helped it survive all those years, but living inside armor is chilly. In the morning, red-eared turtles will warm themselves in the sun.

Red-eared turtle

On land, snapping turtles will strike at anything that comes by—and some types of snapping turtles grow to three feet and weigh over a hundred pounds! You may be happy that these fierce reptiles rarely leave the water. In the security of the water, it uses its extendable neck, powerful jaws, and hooked beak only to attack things small enough to eat.

Like all reptiles, however, snappers come ashore to bury their clutch of leathery eggs in dry ground.

Snapping turtle

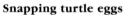
Snapping turtle eggs

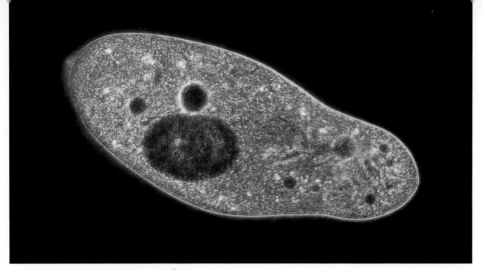

Paramecium

Although you need a microscope to see them, tiny drifting plants and animals known as plankton outnumber all the other pond inhabitants. Many kinds of plankton live in every pond, and a single drop of water may contain thousands.

All the internal parts in the single-cell paramecium can be seen through its transparent skin. The large, dark oval is called the nucleus. It controls many of the animal's activities.

Spyrogyra form soft masses that float on the pond surface. These algae have green spiral bands (called chloroplasts) that turn sunlight into food for the plant.

Spyrogyra

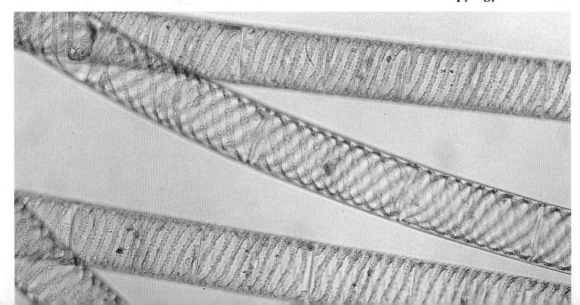

An amoeba moves by constantly changing shape. It pushes "false feet," or pseudopods, in whatever direction it wants to go.

Desmids are one-celled green algae that can look like stars, rods, balls, ovals, or figure-eights. In great numbers, they may tint the water green.

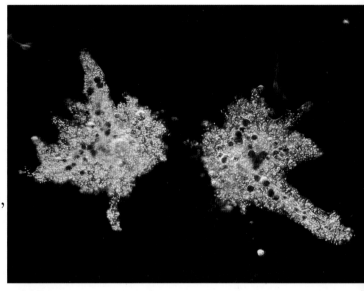

Amoeba

Desmids

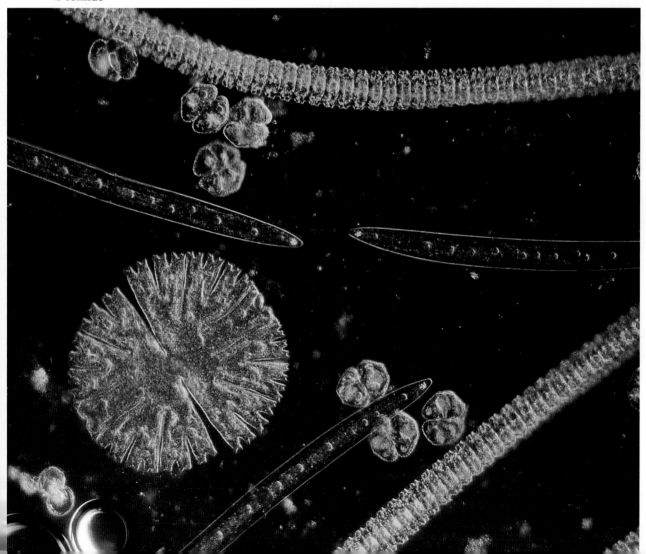

A small creature that feeds on plankton is the waterflea. By the millions, tiny waterfleas occupy all kinds of still water, from ditches to ponds to large lakes. A waterflea swims by paddling one of its two pairs of antennae. As clear as glass, the waterflea reveals all its internal organs, including a yellowish heart that pumps colorless blood.

Waterflea

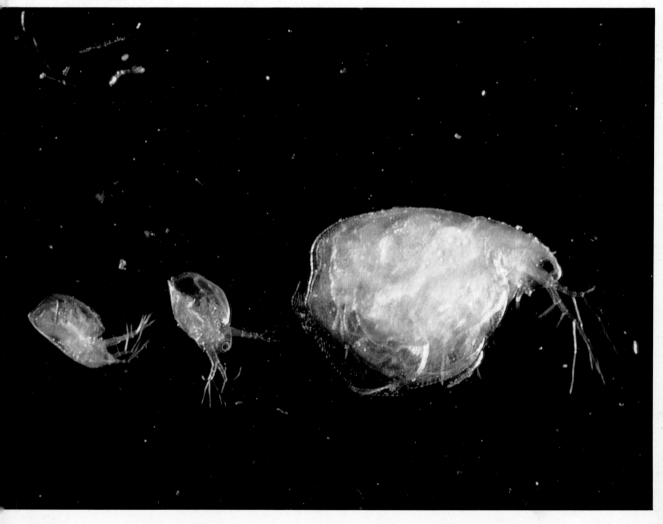

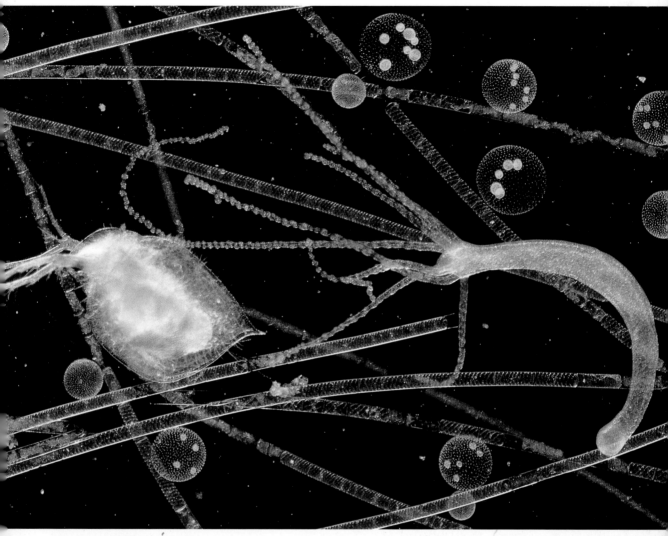

Hydra catching waterflea

Another actor in the pond's cast of miniature characters is the tubelike hydra, an animal that looks a little like an inside-out umbrella. It has special stinging cells to paralyze its prey—here a waterflea. Hydras are about one-fourth of an inch long (large enough to see without a microscope) but you probably won't notice one. As soon as it sees you, it contracts into an unrecognizable blob.

Motionless as a statue, the heron looks peaceful and calm but every muscle is flexed, waiting for a careless fish or frog to pass. When that happens, the large bird's long neck will shoot out like lightning, spearing its meal. At a height that can reach four feet or more, great blue herons are among the pond's most visible—and most spectacular—residents.

Great blue heron

In autumn, birds like the heron begin to migrate south for the winter. The red-winged blackbird is one of the last birds to leave its summer home.

Red-winged blackbird

Frozen pond

Although birds can fly to where it's warmer, other animals can't leave. By the time winter's chill has set in, almost all the pond's inhabitants have changed their lives in some way to cope with the cold. Many insects and small animals die, leaving only their eggs behind.

Bullfrog

Other animals live through the winter by becoming inactive. Frogs and turtles bury themselves in the mud where the frost can't reach. Their heartbeat and breathing slow down so they don't need much oxygen.

Young snapping turtle

Cattail in winter

Some plants (cattails and trees, for instance) may stand the whole winter long. Others die completely, leaving seeds that can survive the cold and begin growing when the warmth of spring arrives once again.